What Does It Take To Be A STAR?

Author:
By Rennie Curran
and
Eleana Curran

Pictures by: Dylan Ross

Published by: Game Changer Ga LLC.
Cover art and Illustrations © DylanRossArt.com
Cover Design by: I Stand Media Group/Visions II Life, Will Cherry
Editing by: Chanda Bell, Joan Darkortey
Curran, Rennie, 2017 – What Does It Take To Be A Star
Library of Congress Control Number:
ISBN: 9780692919156

www.renniecurran.com
Twitter @RennieCurran53
Instagram @RennieCurran
Youtube - Liberiandream35
Facebook - RennieCurran53

First Edition
Printed in United States

SPECIAL THANKS TO:

David, Tube, Chanda, Lesley, Jon and Malcolm.

1

There once was a young boy who dreamed of becoming famous. "What would it take to be a star?" he wondered.

3

One day he came up with a plan.
"I will visit all of the famous people I look
up to the most and ask them what it takes
to be a star."

On Monday, he went to a football game. The stadium was filled with excited fans.

He watched in awe as his favorite player scored again and again. "Touchdown!" the announcer yelled as the crowd erupted in cheers. At the end of the game, the boy saw the football player signing autographs. "What does it take to be a star?" he asked.

The football player looked at the boy with excitement and said, "Meet me here tomorrow morning and I will show you."

On Tuesday morning, the boy met him bright and early at the stadium. This time no one was there.

The football player looked at the young boy and said, "In order to be a star you must work hard when nobody is watching."

The boy thanked the football player for his time and continued on his journey.

In the evening, the boy visited a concert and was blown away by the singer who left the crowd amazed with her voice.

At the end of the concert he saw her standing by her tour bus taking pictures with fans and asked, "What does it take to be a star?"

She looked at him with a smile while she wrote an address on a piece of paper. Then she said, "Meet me at my recording studio."

The boy arrived at the studio to find the singer inside and waiting for him. She seemed exhausted from the long performance.

In a calm voice she said, "In order to be a star you must practice self-control. As a musician, learning to control your tone is very important.

You must know when to use your outside voice and when to use your inside voice."

On Wednesday, the boy went to visit his favorite doctor for a check-up. He was the most well-known doctor in the city. The waiting room was filled with sick people in need of help and he thought to himself, "Everyone is here to see the doctor.
I guess he is kind of famous too."

The boy watched as the doctor greeted everyone with a smile and did his best to help each one of them.

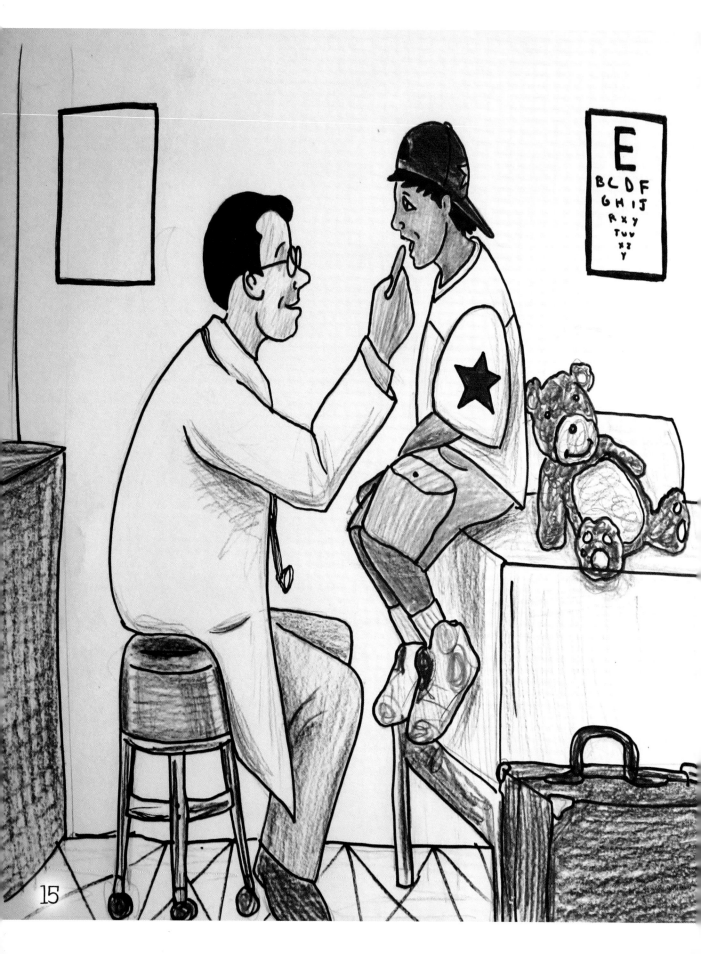

So when it was his turn to visit the doctor
he asked him,
"What does it take to be a star?"

The doctor looked at the boy with joy in his
eyes and said, "Well, I'm not sure I am one,
but if I had to guess I'd say that to be a
star you must be respectful and caring
towards others."

On Thursday, the boy visited the local fire station and the fire fighters were busy preparing to put out a fire.

He followed their truck to see them in action!

19

After they put out the fire, the boy followed them back to the fire station and asked, "What does it take to be a star?"

One firefighter replied, "In order to be a star you must be willing to serve others and think of others before you think of yourself!"

On Friday, the boy visited an art show to see the most famous artist in the city. The audience was amazed by the beautiful artwork he created.

The boy waited
patiently to speak to the artist.
After everyone was gone he asked, "What
does it take to be a star?"

The artist quickly responded, "My dear boy,
to be a star you must understand that
every masterpiece takes time."

"I've never really thought about that before,"
the boy said as he thanked the artist for his
time.

On Saturday, the boy visited his favorite comedian.
The comedian was performing a show and told jokes until everyone had tears in their eyes from laughing so hard.

After the comedy show the boy asked,
"What does it take to be a star?"

The comedian looked at him and said, "To be
a star you must be able to be happy
and laugh even when
no one is laughing with you."

"That must be very hard," the boy noted as
he went on his way.

On Sunday, the boy made his way
over to a marathon race
to catch a very popular runner.

She was very famous and had just
won a gold medal.
"If anyone knows what it takes to be a star,
she will," he concluded.

When the boy saw her he asked, "What does it take to be a star?"

The runner was out of breath, but looked at the boy and said, "In order to be a star you must be able to run towards your dreams, one step at a time, no matter how long it takes. You just keep putting one foot in front of the other!"

The boy left wondering whether he had what it would take to become a star.

It had been a long week. The sun was beginning to set and the stars began to shine. He looked up and saw the biggest star in the sky.

At that moment he realized, "A star is already a star. It doesn't need to figure out how to become one and it doesn't need permission to shine."

"Perhaps," he thought to himself, "a star is not something I should hope to become. Maybe it's something I already am!"
The boy began to shout with excitement, "I am a star! I am a star!"

But thanks to his journey, he now understood he would have to shine brightly for the world to see him and that was something he was going to have to work very hard to achieve!

You are a star!

How will you shine brightly for the world to see you?

About Rennie Curran, Author

Rennie is a former professional athlete, keynote speaker, author, and musician from Atlanta, Georgia who uses his platform to inspire audiences to overcome obstacles, stay ahead of the competition, and reach their fullest potential. His experiences of overcoming many circumstances to reach his childhood dream of becoming three-time All American at The University of Georgia, a 3rd round draft pick in the 2010 NFL Draft, and transitioning into starting his own business gives him a unique perspective on what it takes to handle adversity and maximize opportunities while having a positive impact on others. Through his innovative presentations he teaches people and organizations how to transform their lives and their businesses through leadership and personal development.

Rennie has been counseling and inspiring people for many years. In 2013 he published a motivational self-help book entitled "'Free Agent' The Perspectives of a Young African American Athlete." This motivational self-help book discusses how to overcome adversity and times of transition that we all face along our journey to achieve our dreams.

He has been featured on USA Today, Fox Sports, ESPN College GameDay and The Huffington Post.

When Rennie is not speaking, coaching, or writing he is usually catching up on one his favorite hobbies: music. He grew up playing the piano, drums, and viola. He is also a public servant who spends lots of time giving back through several organizations including: Boys and Girls Club, Fellowship of Christian Athletes, ALS Foundation, Boys Scouts of America, LEDI Liberia, and many more!

Rennie is available for speaking engagements, appearances, camps, commencement speeches, and more!

Website: Renniecurran.com

Instagram: @renniecurran

Twitter: @renniecurran53

Email: info@renniecurran.com

About Eleana Curran, Co-Author

Eleana is a student, soccer player, and author born in Athens, Georgia. Her favorite things to do are play soccer and watch movies. Her favorite food is Sushi. She attends Spalding Drive Elementary School and her favorite subject in school is Math. She is inspired most by her family.

About Dylan Ross, Illustrator

Dylan is an emerging self-taught artist from Douglas, Georgia. Institutions and celebrities worldwide including athletes such as: Dennis Rodman, Lennox Lewis, and Draymond Green have collected his paintings. He currently works out of his hometown studio with representation in New York City and Miami as well as abroad in Dortmund and Düsseldorf, Germany.